Domain Driven Design

How to Easily Implement Domain Driven Design - A Quick & Simple Guide

Table of Contents

Introduction.. 3

Chapter 1: What is Domain Driven Design? 4

Chapter 2: How to Build Domain Knowledge 9

Chapter 3: The Importance of Communication and a Common
Language 12

Chapter 4: What is a Model-Driven Design? 18

Chapter 5: Building Blocks of a Model-Driven Design 21

Chapter 6: Refactoring Towards Deeper Insight 28

Chapter 7: Glossary of Terms 30

Conclusion...32

Introduction

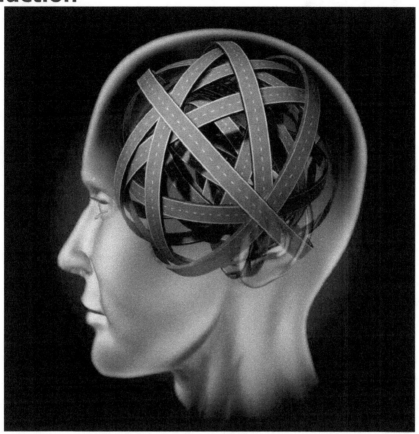

I want to thank you and congratulate you for downloading the book, *"Domain Driven Design: How to Easily Implement Domain Driven Design - A Quick & Simple Guide"*.

This book contains proven steps and strategies on how you can implement the domain-driven design approach in your projects to bring out better results. Through the domain-driven design approach, you and your project team will better understand the domain that you aim to serve and communicate in a common language that can ensure harmony and team work with your group. You will be able to finish the whole design and development process focused on what is truly essential.

Thanks again for downloading this book, I hope you enjoy it!

Chapter 1: What is Domain Driven Design?

Computer software is normally developed in order to automate the different processes that we go through every day including those improvements that advance business processes. Those business processes or the real life problems are the "domain" of the computer software that aims to automate or solve them. If you want to study Domain Driven Design, your understanding should be founded on that concept that computer software is derived from and is totally connected to its domain. A lot of software programmers fail in their endeavors because they focus too much on the codes that make up the software without focusing enough on its domain.

To better understand the concept, let us use the creation of a car as a metaphor. A lot of workers are involved in the creation of the car and many of them specialize in creating specific parts of the car. But because those workers only focus on specific parts, they frequently have an incomplete view of the whole creation process. Most often, they view the car as merely a collection of various parts that they need to interconnect. What those workers do not understand is that the car is much greater than its individual parts. A car that will be well accepted by the consumers actually begins from the designer's vision. The designer will have to meticulously write the car's specifications that will match his vision. From that vision and specification, the designer continues to improve the design by changing and polishing the specifications until they reach perfection and become the true reflection of what the designer has originally envisioned. But do not think that the design process all happens merely on paper. A big part of the process involves the creation of replicas of the actual car so the designer can test whether the car will function as designed. Further modifications are done based on the results of various tests. The car will only be submitted for actual production when all tests have been successfully passed. Only during that time will the various parts be created and put together.

Development of a computer goes through the same process. As a programmer, you are not expected to just sit in front of the computer and type away program codes. Well, of course you can choose to do that and it may actually work for minor projects. But I can tell you that it will rarely work when the project involved is huge and complex.

So that you will be able to design high quality software, you need to understand what that particular software is all about. You cannot really produce an effective software for a banking system if you do not have a working knowledge of the banking industry and how things work. You need to grasp the domain of your software which is the banking industry. The question now is who then understands the banking industry? Is it the architect of the computer software? Not really. Most probably, the most that the software architect knows about banking is how to deposit funds to his bank account, withdraw money from an ATM and issue a check. The answer is not even the software analyst who may be an expert in analyzing any particular topic but he has to be provided all the necessary data and information first before he can perform the analysis. No, it is not also the system developer. The answer, of course, is the bankers themselves. Who else has better understanding of the banking system other than the people who work within the system? The bankers are the subject matter experts and they are familiar with all the fundamentals of the banking system including the rules, catches, issues and solutions to those issues. Therefore, if you want to understand the domain of a banking system software, you need to start talking to the bankers themselves.

When you start a software undertaking, you need to focus on the specific domain that the software will be operating in. Remember, the main objective of the software that you will create is to improve the business processes of a particular domain. You will only be able to achieve that objective if your software can fit closely with the particular domain that the software was designed for. When the contrary happens, the new software will just induce tension in the domain which can ultimately lead to malfunctions and damages.

The question now is how to create that software that can fit closely with the particular domain it was intended for? The most effective way to perform this is to create the software as an expression of the domain. Your software will have to integrate the principal principles and components of the domain and to accurately manifest the various relationships that exist within the domain. Your software should become a model of the domain. If you have no knowledge of the banking system, for instance, you need to learn as much information as he can by reading the software code as a model of the domain. If you don't, your software will not be able to respond properly to different scenarios once it is fully implemented.

What is the next step after you have studied the domain? Always remember that a domain is a specific thing that belongs to our world. You cannot simply take a domain and pour it over the computer keyboard to create your software code. Everything that you have learned from the domain experts will not be simple to convert into software constructs. You will have to produce an abstraction or a blueprint of the domain. At the start, it is understandable that your blueprint of the domain will still be imperfect. As mentioned, you will have to go through several reviews, reviews and testings before you can finally perfect the design of your software. As you go through these steps, your abstraction will become clearer and more defined.

Putting Domain Model to Work

The abstraction that you need to create is basically a model of the domain you want to create the software for. As maintained by Eric Evans, "a domain model is not a particular diagram; it is the idea that the diagram is intended to convey". The domain model is not merely the stored knowledge in the head of the domain expert. Instead, it is a meticulously organized and discerning abstraction of that stored knowledge. A domain model can be represented by or communicated through a diagram, a written code and even plain English sentences.

The domain model will become your internal depiction of the targeted domain and it will play an important role all throughout the process of designing and developing the software. The human mind is not really capable of storing and processing loads of information. You will need to sort out and organize that information so you can apportion them into smaller chunks of information that can be grouped into rational modules that you can tackle one at a time. When you start designing the process, you will be able to refer to the model to improve your design. A domain model is a vital element of your software design. You will need it for you to be able to manage the complexities the design. Your thoughts during the design process can be integrated to the domain model so you can squeeze out of your head all the possible ideas you can implement for the software.

After you have completed your domain model, you need to share your model with other people who have interests on the software including the domain experts and the other designers and developers within your group. The software design in your head should be accurately and completely conveyed to the other project shareholders to avoid any ambiguities. You can communicate your domain model through different media including diagrams, pictures, drawings, narratives and language among others.

After your domain model has been clearly communicated with other shareholders, you can then begin creating the code design for your software. Maybe you are aware that code designing is different from software designing. We can compare software designing to the creation of a house's architecture which focuses on the big picture. Code designing, on the other hand, focuses on the details of the house design such as the position of specific paintings on a particular wall. Code designing is a vital step in the creation of a software but it is not as essential as software designing. Normally, the mistakes committed during code design can be corrected without much trouble but any errors or mistakes in the software design can be very expensive to correct or repair. So it is vital that you spend enough time in the creation of the overall design of your software through the process of building and refining your domain model.

Chapter 2: How to Build Domain Knowledge

To illustrate how you can build domain knowledge, let assume that you are assigned to create a software for the monitoring and control system that can track all airplane flights over a particular location. The software will help determine if a particular plane is flying through its specified route or if there are possibilities of collision.

Now, you will ask yourself where you can begin gaining a good perspective of the domain for the domain development which is air traffic control. In the previous chapter, we said that you should talk with the subject matter or domain experts to gain a good understanding of the domain. In our example, the domain experts are the air traffic controllers. But when you talk to them, you need to understand that the air traffic controllers may be experts in their domain but they are not experienced or trained in system or software design. So do not expect that the domain experts can provide you with a comprehensive account of the problem domain.

Yes, the controllers have an extensive familiarity of the air traffic control domain but in order for you to create your domain model, you will have to pull out all the necessary information that you need so you can generalize them. When you begin your discussions with the controllers, you will most probably hear lots of information about airplane take offs and landings, the dangers of collision and other facts and information. In order for you to put some order in a discussion that can turn out chaotic, you need to know the right place to start. You need to first define the key function of the domain and then create a process map that will outline the flow of activities and transactions within the domain.

At the start, you and the controller may agree on the three main elements of the domain which are the airplane, a departure location and a destination. You will then have to learn what happens to the airplane while it is airborne and flying to the destination. The air traffic controller will then explain to you how each airplane is appointed a specific flight plan that reflects all the details of the whole travel. You will then hear about how each airplane has to follow a certain route. With this additional information, your perspective of the air travel will expand from just the departure point and destination point to include the actual route that the plane has to travel.

After further discussion, you will also learn that each of the routes that the planes follow is further divided into several smaller segments which when connected to one another comprise a curved line that starts from the departure point and ends at the destination point. As you continue talking to the controller, you also learn that the line passes through several fixed points that have been predetermined. With that you realize that the plane route is actually a sequence of successive fixed points and that the departure and destination points are not really terminal points but are basically two of those fixed points.

All throughout your discussions, you are expected to create diagrams that you revise and refine as you learn more facts and information about the domain. You need to ask the right questions to the domain expert so they will be able to respond with the correct information. The ideas and concepts that may emerge from your discussions may sound coarse and disordered by they are quite important for you to better understand the domain.

The output of your discussion with the domain expert is a domain model that reflects the vital elements of the domain and is an essential part of the whole software design. At this point, you can start building an initial prototype of the software so you can see how things work thus far. When you do that, you will note that issues will surface which may require you to do revision and refinements on the model. It is ideal that at this point, you present your early prototype to the domain experts, the software architects and the system developers so they can give you additional feedback that can help in the refinement of your domain model. The process of creating and refining your domain model may seem tedious and time consuming but you need to accept that that is the ideal process that you should perform to ensure that the software that you will create will be able to effectively provide solutions to the real problems and issues of the domain.

Chapter 3: The Importance of Communication and a Common Language

In the first two chapters, you learned the importance of developing a domain model and how you can create one by working closely with domain experts. This approach is ideal but it can cause some preliminary struggles because of communication barriers between the software specialist and the domain expert. As a software developer, it is expected that your mind is full of terminologies such as class, method, algorithm and pattern. You are also inclined to always look for a connection between real life concepts and programming artifacts. You are always trying to discern what types of object class you can create and what types of relationships you can use to model those object classes. On the other hand, the domain experts are not really expected to understand any of the things that you like to think and talk about. They do not really care much what a software library means or a framework, persistence or even seemingly common words such as database. But despite that, you cannot discount the fact that they are experts in their own fields.

In our previous example, for instance, the air traffic controllers are experts when it comes to airplanes and their routes. They know about altitude, longitude and latitude, trajectories and deviations from normal routes. They are very comfortable speaking their own jargon which can seem confusing to outsiders who are not really familiar with the domain.

To rise above this disparity in communication style while building your domain model, you need to learn how to communicate with the domain expert so you will be able to effectively share ideas about the domain model and its various components. You need to realize how important effective communication is at this particular level in your software development. Without an effective communication system, you and the domain expert may not be able to understand what you are explaining to each other which can ultimately lead to the failure of your project.

Just like any other team, your project team will face severe problems and issues when the members of the team cannot communicate through a common language. The terms used in daily discussions are normally detached from the terms embedded in the software code which in the end is considered as the main product part of the computer software project. You may have also noticed that even you can use diverse languages in your speech and in your writings. Most often, the most insightful representations of a particular domain can appear in an ephemeral form but can never be encapsulated in the software code or even in simple writing.

When you are holding discussions with the domain experts and other members of the project team, the use of translation is crucial to ensure that everyone understands the concepts and ideas in a similar manner. Software developers sometimes attempt to explicate the patterns in the software design using the language of a layman but more often than not, they do so without much success. The domain experts, on the other hand, will endeavor to explain the intricacies of the domain by crafting new jargons which in the end adds more confusion to the process. Now, you may already agree that there really is a need for a common language when you want to implement domain driven design. But you may also ask which language should the team use? Should it be language of the developers or the domain experts?

Another central principle of domain driven design that you need to understand is the use of a language that is founded on the domain model itself. Given that the domain model is the common ground between the software developers and the domain experts, it is but natural to make it a common place where the software and the domain can meet and jive.

The domain model itself is used as the foundation of the common language. To make sure that your project will succeed, you need to constantly appeal to all members of the team to use the common language not only in all communications within the team but in the software code itself. During the whole process of software design and development, all members of the project team will be sharing their thoughts, knowledge and ideas as everyone tries to refine and enhance the domain model. The whole team will have several discussions, written narratives and various diagrams. You need to make sure that the common language is consistently used in all these forms of communications. Because of this characteristic, this common language is also referred to as "Ubiquitous" language, meaning it is everywhere and always present.

The Ubiquitous Language will enable you to connect all of the elements of the design and to create the foundation from for the design project team to perform effectively. You may already be aware that software project designs in large scale can take several weeks or probably months to complete. At the start of the project, you and the team will be defining the fundamental concepts of the project. But as you continue to work on the project, the team members will realize that some of their early concepts were erroneous or inappropriate so revisions and refinements need to be done and new components of the software design has to be deliberated to fit into the general design of the software. All these activities will really be hard to pull off successfully if the project team does not share a common language.

Languages cannot really be developed overnight. It will take some effort and lots of motivation to ensure that all the vital components of the language are uncovered. But your job will be to discover what those vital components that identify both the domain and the software design are. After you have identified those vital components, you will then need to look for the appropriate words to use for those vital components. Some of the appropriate words can be effortlessly recognized but others will be quite more difficult.

As you build the common language, you will have to settle several difficulties through experimentations with different alternative expressions until you find the most appropriate words that would reflect the alternative domain model. The next steps include refactoring the codes and giving new names to the various classes, methods and modules to ensure that they match the new domain model. You will have to spend some time resolving confusions through conversations with the team members much the same way you will decide on the meanings of everyday words. When you build your ubiquitous language in that process, you are almost sure to come out with a domain model and a common language that are clearly consistent with each other. Every time there will be changes to the common language, the same change should be done on the domain model.

You need to emphasize to the domain experts that they also play a crucial role in building both the common language and the domain model itself. They should feel empowered enough to raise objections against terminologies or structures that seem problematic or deficient in conveying the true nature of the domain. If the domain experts cannot comprehend some terminologies in the language or structures in the domain model, it most likely means that there is something that needs to be revised or refined. Similarly, the software developers should also feel empowered enough to voice out any ambiguities or inconsistencies that appear in the software design.

All members of the team should be conscious of the necessity to build a common language and they should always be prompted to maintain their focus on the most essential aspects of the project and to use the common language as often as possible. The different members of the team who basically belong to different fields should limit the use of their own jargon so that the Ubiquitous Language will properly evolve and flourish.

In addition, it is ideal for the software developers to apply the primary concepts of the domain model in the code that they are creating. They have the option of writing separate classes for different model concepts so they can easily map not only between the domain model and the code but also between the common language and the code. This is particularly beneficial in making the code clearer and more comprehensible when reproducing the domain model. This effort will also pay off when the domain model expands to larger proportions and corresponding changes in the code need to be done.

The ubiquitous language is not only good as a foundation for the creation of the domain model. It is also a very useful tool in writing down a vital concept as a class and to convey relationships between those classes. When preparing for a discussion with the whole team, you can easily sketch 4 or 5 different classes on your sketchpad, jot down their tags and illustrate the relationships between those classes. That way, everyone will be able to easily follow your thought process. With your graphical illustration of your idea, everyone in the team can immediately share your vision about a particular topic and discussions will flow much better after that. When new concepts and ideas crop up during the discussion, you can easily modify your diagrams to manifest the change in concept.

UML diagrams are very useful when the elements involved are limited in number. But watch out because you may get so used to them that they eventually overwhelm you. It can really be overwhelming when you have tens or even hundreds of classes depicted as diagrams. Software developers may find it very difficult and confusing to go through all through those diagrams. And you can imagine how more difficult and confusing it can be for domain experts. Do not attempt to use it for projects that are medium to large sized because it may only defeat the purpose.

Another limitation of UML diagrams is that they cannot really effectively convey the meanings of the concepts that they represent and what the various objects in the diagram are assumed to do. But you do not have to worry about that because you can use other communication tools to bridge those gaps. For one, you can use documentations. An option to communicate your model is create smaller diagrams that contain a subset of the whole domain model.

Each of those smaller diagrams can then contain a number of classes and how the classes are related to one another. With the small diagrams, you will already be able to include a decent fraction of all the concepts involved in your model. After that, you can then add texts to your diagrams which can give more details on the behaviors and constraints that the diagrams cannot convey. If it will be easier for you, you can create these documents manually by drawing and writing by hand. Since your diagrams are only drafts, you can easily transmit your thoughts and ideas on papers when you create them by hand.

Chapter 4: What is a Model-Driven Design?

In the previous chapters, you have learned the significance of the domain driven design approach for software developers. When you have domain model that accurately reflects the vital elements of the domain, you will be able to create a software that provide real solutions to the problems and issues in the domain. You also understood the necessity of having a ubiquitous language that can help make effective communication amongst all members of the project team possible. Now it is time for you to learn how to implement the domain model in your codes which is also a vital stage in the process of software development. Even if you have a impressive model, you can never really say your project is successful unless you can effectively transform that model into your software code.

It is expected that a software analyst will work closely with the business domain experts for several weeks or months to come up with a domain model that can accurately capture the fundamental concepts of the domain. After both the software and the domain experts are fairly satisfied with the domain model, it will then be forwarded to the software developers who will then examine the model to determine how to proceed with the coding process. It is possible that the software developer will realize that there are certain concepts or relationships in the model that cannot be accurately stated in the code. What normally happens is that the software developer will take the liberty to add their own ideas to the domain model in developing the software codes. The developer may choose to put additional classes which can ultimately widen the gap between the original domain model and the final software implementation. Because of that, it cannot always be guaranteed that the final result will be a good one. There are instances when the final products cannot really prevail through the tests of time and that end users find that they are very difficult to maintain. It is therefore very critical that you apply the proper approach in transforming your domain model into codes.

A good approach is to directly correlate the domain model with the design. The software analyst should construct the domain model with the understanding that he or she needs to consider the software and design processes into the model. The software developers should be involved in the process of creating the model so that the outcome will be a model that can be suitably expressed in software codes. With that, the developers will not be tempted to make their own revisions of the model and the design process will then become clear-cut and fully based on the domain model. When the software codes are tightly related to the fundamental model, the codes will have meaning that can make the model more significant. When developers are also highly involved during the creation of the model, the software analysts can receive instant feedback that will allow them to immediately make the proper revisions.

When the software developers are involved in the creation of the model, they will feel more responsible for it and they will feel keener to maintain its integrity. Before they even try to add changes to the code, their instinct will be to change the domain model itself. Because they feel more responsible for the model, they will avoid refactoring the codes up to the point where the codes no longer reflects the original domain model. It is also important that the software analyst is involved in the implementation process to make sure that he is always aware of the limitations that were uncovered during software development. The software analyst will be able to work with the developers in revising the model to work around those limitations.

If the software design or a major part of it cannot be mapped to the original domain model, it can mean that the model itself has an insignificant value which can lead people to doubt the appropriateness of the software itself. But on the other end, complicated mappings between the domain model and the design functions can also prove to be as damaging because it will be very impractical to maintain the codes as the design is changed over time. One way to work around these limitations is to design a segment of the software system in such a way that it can mirror the domain model in a precise manner which will then make mapping quite evident. The software analyst should also constantly re-examine the domain model so that he can create the proper revisions and modifications that can then be applied more naturally to the software code. All the members of the team should strive to end up with one single domain model that can be upheld until the end of the project as much as they strive to support a fluent common language shared by all. The software developers should be able to extract from the domain model the terminologies that they will be using in the design and in creating the assignment of fundamental responsibilities. With that, the software code will then become an ultimate expression of the domain model.

In order to firmly bind the code implementation to the domain model, you will normally require software development tools and languages that can sustain the modeling paradigm. One example of these tools is object-oriented programming which is ideal for model implementation mainly because both object-oriented programming and model implementation are founded on similar paradigms. Object-oriented programming (OOP) can provide the classes, associations, object instances and object messaging that are require in model implementation. OOP can also facilitate the direct mapping between a model object with other relationships and counterparts in programming.

Chapter 5: Building Blocks of a Model-Driven Design

Layered Architecture

When a software application is created, a big portion of it is normally not directly correlated to the business domain but is instead a component of the infrastructure that supports the software itself. It is also expected that the part of an application that is related to the domain is comparatively smaller because an application will typically contain lots of other codes for access controls to the database, files and networks and for user interface.

Software developers normally write the codes for these user interfaces, database, object-oriented programs and other support codes directly to the business objects themselves. These various layers can get mixed up with the codes that are related to the domain itself which can make the domain quite difficult to make out and think about. Any superficial alterations in the user interface can ultimately alter the business logic. In order for a programmer to make the required alterations in the business rule or logic, he will have to meticulously trade those alterations from the user interface codes, database codes and other elements of the program. In the end, it may be very impractical to implement model-driven objects that remain coherent. Even the automated tests on the program may become uncoordinated.

Because each of the activities in the program involves a lot of technology and logic, it is highly advisable to keep the program especially uncomplicated and straightforward to avoid confusion and ultimate breakdown. A complicated program should be divided into several layers where a design can be developed within each of the layers. Each layer design should be consistent with the other layers surrounding it. To afford free coupling with the layers above, you should create a standard architectural pattern. Assemble and converge all of the domain model-related codes into a single layer so you can separate it from the codes related to user interfaces, applications and infrastructures. You can focus the expression of the domain model on the domain objects that are not required to be displayed, stored or even managed in application tasks. Doing this will let your domain model to freely evolve to become loaded and clear enough to encapsulate vital business information that can be put to work.

A domain-driven design normally includes four conceptual layers: user interface (or the presentation layer), application layer, domain layer and infrastructure layer.

- The user interface is in charge of showing the program information to the various users and translating the various commands given by the users.

- The application layer synchronizes all of the application activities. It normally doesn't involve business rules or logic. It also doesn't hold the status of the various business objects but it can hold the status of the progress of application tasks.

- As derived from its name, the domain layer holds all the information about the business domain and it is usually considered as the center of the computer software. This is where the status of the business objects is held.

- The infrastructure layer functions as the support library for all of the three other layers. It enables the other layers to effective communicate with each other. It also enables the implementation of the persistence for the business objects.

Entities

There is a specific group of object that has a consistent identity throughout the various states of the software program. For these particular of objects, what matters the most is the thread of their continuity and identity instead of their individual attributes. The thread of continuity and identity of these objects can actually span the complete life of the program and can even continue further than the program's life. These objects are referred to as Entities.

Languages for object-oriented programming store the object instances in their memories and they link a memory address or reference for each of the program objects. The references are typically unique at any particular time but there is no assurance that they will remain unique for an indeterminate time period. Because the various program objects are frequently moved in and out of the memory, they are sequenced and passed on to the network and are either reconstructed at the other end or destroyed. These references which stand as identities for the running environment of the software program are not basically the identities that we are trying to explain. For instance, if there is a particular class that maintains weather information, it is rather likely to have two distinct instances of a particular class with each one holding similar values. These two objects are considered totally equal and exchangeable with each other even if they have dissimilar references. Because of this nature, these objects are not considered as entities.

Value Objects

A programmer may become enticed to create all objects as entities because they can be easily tracked. But you need to understand that the creation and tracking of identities come with a high cost. You will need to ensure that each of the objects has their unique identities and monitoring identities is not really that simple. You also need to be extra careful when deciding what constitutes a particular identity because any wrong decisions can result to different objects having similar identities which you do not really want to happen. The performance of the program can also be greatly affected when all objects are created as entities because you will have to create one instance for all the objects. For example, if you will create "customer" as an entity object, you will need to create one instance for all the customers that will be created. And this could mean hundreds or even thousands of customer files. You will end up with a degradation of the system performance because of the volume of existing instances. This is where the Value Objects come in. Because value object have no unique identities, it is easy for you to both create and discard them.

It is ideal that you create value objects that are absolute and cannot be altered during their entire lifetime. If you later on decide that you require another value for a particular value object, you should not revise the old one but instead create a new one. This process has significant effects in the program design. Because value objects are absolute and have no unique identities, they can be easily shared and exhibit data integrity which is vital for certain program designs.

Services

When you perform the analysis of the business domain and the definition of the primary objects that comprise the domain model, it is highly likely that you will uncover some elements of the domain that cannot be readily mapped to the various objects. The objects in the program are normally deemed to have certain characteristics or internal states that are managed by the object itself and demonstrate particular behaviors. When you create the common language for the project team, the vital elements of the domain are incorporated into the language. In normal circumstances, the nouns in the common language can be readily be mapped into the program objects. The corresponding verbs connected to those nouns also develop as parts of the behaviors of those objects. But there are certain action words or verbs in the domain that may not appear to fit into any of the objects. These action words normally correspond to significant behaviors in the domain so you cannot really choose to neglect them or to merely incorporate them with a certain entity or value object. When you simply add those behaviors into objects, they can ruin the object itself by letting stand for functionalities that do not really belong to those objects.

When you recognize those types of behaviors in the business domain that you are working on, your best option is to declare them as a "service" which is basically a program object that doesn't have its own internal state. The primary purpose of a service is to give functionality to the domain. The role that a service plays in the whole program is a vital one because it can assemble functionalities that are related to one another so they provide service to various entities and value object. It is ideal to state the Service unambiguously in order to create an obvious distinction in the domain that clearly represents the vital concepts.

Modules

A domain model can grow extremely big especially when it involves a huge and complicated application. The domain model can reach a point where it will be difficult to talk about it in its entirety. It may be very difficult to understand how all the various parts of the domain relate and interact with one another. Because of that, it is important that you are able to systematize your domain into separate modules which you can use to organize interrelated concepts and activities to trim down the complexity of your application.

When you use modules in your projects, you will find it easier to see the complete picture of your domain model by looking at the modules separately and then looking at how those different modules are interrelated. Once you have a good understanding of how the different modules are interrelated, you can then move on to deciphering the details within each module.

Aggregates, Factories and Repositories

The various objects in the domain can undergo an array of states during their entire life cycle. The objects are first created then nested in a memory, used in calculations and eventually destroyed when they will no longer be used. There are certain instances when the objects have to be saved in a permanent database or an archive so they can be easily retrieved at a later time. But it can still be decided that these objects be totally removed from the system both in the active database and storage for archives.

The management of an object's life cycle can pose some challenges to the software administrators. If this is not done correctly, it may have negative effect on the entire domain model. There are three common patterns that can help facilitate the management of the life cycle of various domain objects: aggregates, factories and repositories. Aggregates are domain patterns that are utilized to identify the ownership and boundaries of an object. Factories and repositories, on the other hand, are design patterns that facilitate the management of creation and storage of the domain objects.

An aggregate is a collection of related domain objects that are regarded as a single unit in terms of data changes. The aggregate is separated by a boundary line that segregates the internal objects from the external ones. Every aggregate has a single root which is an entity. This entity is the only object that can be accessed from the outside of the aggregate. That particular root contains references to all of the objects in the aggregate. Each of the objects in the aggregate can contain references to one another but any object from the outside can contain references to the root object only.

An aggregate can ensure the integrity of program data and enforce invariants primarily because external objects can contain references to the root object only which indicates that the external objects are not capable of directly altering the other objects within the aggregate. The external objects can only alter the root object or command the root object to execute certain actions. The root object is capable of altering other objects but that function can only be executed by the root object within the aggregate which makes the function highly controllable.

Factories are domain patterns that are utilized to sum up all the information required for the creation of an object. Factories are particularly valuable in creating aggregates. When the root object of an aggregate is generated, all of the other objects that will be contained inside the aggregate will simultaneously be created and all of the invariants will also be automatically enforced.

A repository is another domain pattern that has a primary purpose of encapsulating all the logic and rules required to obtain the various object references. Because of repositories, the different domain objects will not have to directly deal with the application infrastructure to obtain their required references to the other objects within the entire domain.

Chapter 6: Refactoring Towards Deeper Insight

In the previous chapters, you have understood the value of building a model that accurately represents the business domain you want to build the software for. You have also recognized the importance of designing the codes around the domain model and that the model itself needs to be revised and refined based on changes done during the code design. Software codes that were designed without a model can result to software that cannot truly provide solutions to the problems of the domain it aims to serve. On the other hand, when a domain model is done without getting timely feedbacks from the software designers and developers can result to a domain model that is not fully understood by everyone who is involved in the completion of the software project.

While the process of designing and developing the software is progressing, you will have to stop once in a while in order to take a look at how the code is forming. There will be times when you have to decide that it is time to perform a refactoring which is the process of revamping the design of the code to enhance it without altering the overall behavior of the application. Refactoring is normally done in little steps to ensure that they are controllable and will not go out of hand. Small refactoring steps can ensure that the functionalities of the application will not breakdown or that bugs are not introduced into the system. Remember, the objective of the refactoring process is to improve your code and not to make it worse. Regular tests that are automated is ideally performed to make certain that nothing was broken or damaged during the refactoring.

There are several methods to perform code refactoring. And there are also several refactoring patterns that you can use. A refactoring pattern is basically an automated strategy in refactoring. There are tools incorporated on those refactoring patterns that can help your life as a software developer a lot easier compared to the more traditional methods. The modern refactoring patterns deal directly with the code itself and its quality.

Another kind of refactoring is directly connected to the domain and the domain model. There will be instances when new insights about the domain will appear or when particular elements in the domain model become clearer or certain relationships between two or more components are discovered. All these new discoveries should be incorporated into your code design through the method of refactoring. To be able to do this, it is vital that your expressive codes are simple to read and comprehend. Just based on reading the codes, people should be able to determine not only what the particular codes do but why they do their functions. It is only through this way can your codes truly capture the real essence of your domain model.

One kind of refactoring patterns is referred to as technical refactoring which is highly controlled and structured. You cannot actually perform refactoring that can lead to deeper insights when you do technical refactoring. There are no specific patterns that can be created for refactoring for deeper insight. The intricacies of a domain model cannot really allow refactoring through a mechanistic approach. You will be able to refactor properly if you think deeply and incorporate your and the other team members' insights, experiences and flair.

You also need to make sure that your code design is flexible enough because a rigid design will always resist refactoring. Remember, codes that were not put together without considering flexibility are codes that will be very difficult to work with. Whenever there are changes required, you will realize that you will struggle in every step of the way. You will note that those elements that could have been refactored quite easily will take a longer time and more effort.

Chapter 7: Glossary of Terms

Aggregate
A group of domain objects that are bound jointly by a root entity which is also referred to as aggregate root. The aggregate root ensures that all alterations made inside the aggregate are consistent by making sure that any external domain object is forbidden from containing references to the members of the aggregate.

Domain
A field of knowledge, authority or activities. The domain of a specific software is the specific subject area or field from which the system developers applies the program.

Domain-driven Design
A software development approach that involves deep connection of the software implementation to the highly-evolving model of the core business domain.

Entity
A domain object that is not identified through its own attributes but through its own thread of continuity and its own uniqueness.

Factory
The different methods used to retrieve domain objects are required to be delegated to a dedicated factory object. This is to ensure that an implementation of an alternative storage can be interchanged effortlessly.

Model
A structure of thoughts and ideas that depicts selected facets of a specific domain and can be utilized to resolve problems connected to that particular domain.

Repository
The different methods used to retrieve domain objects are required to be delegated to a dedicated repository object. This is to ensure that an implementation of an alternative storage can be interchanged effortlessly.

Service
A condition where a specific operation in the domain does not theoretically fit in any of the domain objects. By pursuing the innate contours

of the issue or problem, one can apply these operations in the services.

Ubiquitous Language   A common language created around the domain model and employed by all members of the project team to associate all the activities that the team is required to complete.

Value Object   A domain object that includes several attributes but has no theoretical or conceptual identity. They are ideally treated as absolute or immutable.

Conclusion

Thank you again for downloading this book!

I hope this book was able to help you to better understand how the domain driven design approach can improve the output of your software development team.

The next step is to review any of your existing projects to determine how you can apply the concepts you learned in this book.

Thank you and good luck!

www.ingramcontent.com/pod-product-compliance
Lightning Source LLC
Chambersburg PA
CBHW060109090326

40690CB00063B/4352